MW01643776

The Self-Improvement Companion Journal

THE SELF-IMPROVEMENT COMPANION JOURNAL

1st Edition

By Jacob Craig (www.twelvepaths.com)

Created and published by Inspiring Leaders Collective

ISBN 978-1-7363781-9-9 Hardcover Print

To you. May you exceed your own expectations for what you'll accomplish in this next year.

How to Use This Journal

About This Journal

The purpose of this journal is to assist you with setting goals quarterly and weekly, tracking habits daily, and reflecting and planning as you progress through a year's time. It by no means needs to start or end at specific times; feel free to move at your own pace.

This journal includes:

- 4 quarterly assessments to assist with setting goals
- 52 weekly forms for setting weekly goals and tracking daily habits
- 52 writing prompts to invite you to journal at least once weekly
- 52 sheets for open journaling

My one ask is that you are honest with yourself when assessing goals and tracking habits so that you can take best advantage of this journal and, in turn, improve and achieve incredible things. Even if your main goals are simply to have better relationships with your loved ones and to be able to spend more time with them, this journal is here to help you do that.

Thank you for picking up this journal and I hope it exceeds your expectations.

How to Use the Quarterly Assessments

Quarterly Assessments are included to assist you with setting goals. They ask:

1. Your current level of fulfillment in the 5 main categories of life: Relationships, Career, Health & Fitness, Education, and Lifestyle.
2. How you can improve these areas of life.
3. To write down 20 goals.
4. Lastly, to narrow it down to 5 goals maximum to focus on.

My recommendations for setting goals are:

- While setting them, ask yourself which areas of life could use most improvement and which categories are most important to you at the time.
- Use this framework: "I will [accomplishment] by/until [Month, Day, Year]."
    - e.g. "I will call all my siblings once a week until January 1, 2025," could be a Relationships goal.
- Some goals should be easy and some should be challenging.
- Timeframe doesn't matter, they can be longer or shorter than a quarter.

These assessments take some time but don't feel like you can't move on if it's not filled out. Again, move at your own pace. You can always come back to the assessments later on.

How to Use the Weekly Forms

The Weekly Forms included are to assist with setting weekly goals and tracking daily habits. They prompt you to write up to 4 goals and 4 habits to focus on for that week – they could be related to your goals set for that quarter but they don't need to be. There are also questions before the week starts to help forecast difficulties and provide encouragement, and then after to assess how it went.

Here is an example of the habit tracker filled out:

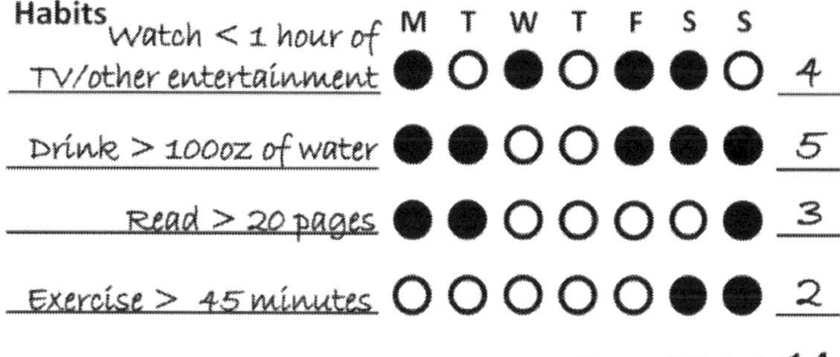

Filling in the circles for each day could be done as you go to bed or the following morning. What qualifies as a "good number" for each habit and for the weekly grand total is left to your own discretion.

This Weekly Form is the core of the journal. They also shouldn't take more than 5 or 10 minutes to complete.

Other Information

This journal is a stand-alone but could also be considered a companion to my upcoming book that is scheduled to release later in 2024.

You can find more information on my blog, www.twelvepaths.com, and sign up for my email list there if you'd like to be notified of the release and any future releases. There potentially could be future editions of this journal if I receive enough feedback.

If you have any questions or want to share any thoughts, ideas, or comments, my email is twelvepathsnews@gmail.com.

Now go complete your first quarterly assessment and weekly form! Happy journaling! ☺

Sincerely,
Jacob Craig
March 12, 2024

Quarter 1

How would you rate your current level of fulfillment in your...

Relationships

Career

Health & Fitness

Education

Lifestyle

What are some ways you could improve the success of your...

Relationships

____

____

____

Career

____

____

____

Health & Fitness

____

____

____

Education

____

____

____

Lifestyle

____

____

____

Write down 20 potential goals:

1. ____

2. ____

3. ____

4. ____

5. ____

6. ____

7. ____

8. ____

9. ____

10. ____

11. ____

12. ____

13. ____

14. ____

15. ____

16. ____

17. ____

18. ____

19. ____

20. ____

And now choose up to 5 to focus on and cross out the rest.

What are your main goals?

Goal #1

____

____

Goal #2

____

____

Goal #3

____

____

Goal #4

____

____

Goal #5

____

____

Weekly Goals & Habit Tracker

Week Start Date: ____ /____ /________

Goals

- O 1. ________________________________
- O 2. ________________________________
- O 3. ________________________________
- O 4. ________________________________

What could get in the way of your goals this week?
Give yourself some words of advice or encouragement.

____

____

Habits	**M**	**T**	**W**	**T**	**F**	**S**	**S**	
____________________	O	O	O	O	O	O	O	___
____________________	O	O	O	O	O	O	O	___
____________________	O	O	O	O	O	O	O	___
____________________	O	O	O	O	O	O	O	___

Grand Total ___

How did the week go? What could you have done better?

____

____

Where do see yourself in 5 years? 10 years?

Weekly Goals & Habit Tracker

Week Start Date: ____ /____ /________

Goals

- ○ 1. ____
- ○ 2. ____
- ○ 3. ____
- ○ 4. ____

What could get in the way of your goals this week?
Give yourself some words of advice or encouragement.

____

____

Habits	**M**	**T**	**W**	**T**	**F**	**S**	**S**	
______________________	○	○	○	○	○	○	○	___
______________________	○	○	○	○	○	○	○	___
______________________	○	○	○	○	○	○	○	___
______________________	○	○	○	○	○	○	○	___

Grand Total ___

How did the week go? What could you have done better?

____

____

Do you find yourself living in the moment more than you plan for your future? Do you feel you need to do one of those more often?

Weekly Goals & Habit Tracker

Week Start Date: ____ /____ /________

Goals

○ 1. ____

○ 2. ____

○ 3. ____

○ 4. ____

What could get in the way of your goals this week?
Give yourself some words of advice or encouragement.

____

____

Habits	**M**	**T**	**W**	**T**	**F**	**S**	**S**	
____________________	○	○	○	○	○	○	○	___
____________________	○	○	○	○	○	○	○	___
____________________	○	○	○	○	○	○	○	___
____________________	○	○	○	○	○	○	○	___

Grand Total ___

How did the week go? What could you have done better?

____

____

Who is someone you look up to? Why?

Weekly Goals & Habit Tracker

Week Start Date: ____ /____ /________

Goals

○ 1. ____

○ 2. ____

○ 3. ____

○ 4. ____

What could get in the way of your goals this week?
Give yourself some words of advice or encouragement.

____

____

Habits	M	T	W	T	F	S	S	
____________________	○	○	○	○	○	○	○	___
____________________	○	○	○	○	○	○	○	___
____________________	○	○	○	○	○	○	○	___
____________________	○	○	○	○	○	○	○	___

Grand Total ___

How did the week go? What could you have done better?

____

____

Do you find yourself spending a lot of time on an activity that could just be a distraction? What are ways you could mitigate that time that's potentially wasted?

Weekly Goals & Habit Tracker

Week Start Date: ____ /____ /________

Goals

- ○ 1. ______________________________
- ○ 2. ______________________________
- ○ 3. ______________________________
- ○ 4. ______________________________

What could get in the way of your goals this week?
Give yourself some words of advice or encouragement.

____

____

Habits	M	T	W	T	F	S	S	
______________	○	○	○	○	○	○	○	___
______________	○	○	○	○	○	○	○	___
______________	○	○	○	○	○	○	○	___
______________	○	○	○	○	○	○	○	___

Grand Total ___

How did the week go? What could you have done better?

____

____

Is there a goal (or multiple goals) you've been trying to reach for a long time? What keeps getting in the way?

Weekly Goals & Habit Tracker

Week Start Date: ____ /____ /________

Goals

- O 1. ____
- O 2. ____
- O 3. ____
- O 4. ____

What could get in the way of your goals this week?
Give yourself some words of advice or encouragement.

____

____

Habits	**M**	**T**	**W**	**T**	**F**	**S**	**S**	
____________________	O	O	O	O	O	O	O	___
____________________	O	O	O	O	O	O	O	___
____________________	O	O	O	O	O	O	O	___
____________________	O	O	O	O	O	O	O	___

Grand Total ___

How did the week go? What could you have done better?

____

____

Who in your life are you grateful for and why? At a minimum, name 4 people.

Weekly Goals & Habit Tracker

Week Start Date: ____ /____ /________

Goals

- O 1. ____
- O 2. ____
- O 3. ____
- O 4. ____

What could get in the way of your goals this week?
Give yourself some words of advice or encouragement.

____

____

Habits	M	T	W	T	F	S	S	
____________________	O	O	O	O	O	O	O	___
____________________	O	O	O	O	O	O	O	___
____________________	O	O	O	O	O	O	O	___
____________________	O	O	O	O	O	O	O	___

Grand Total ___

How did the week go? What could you have done better?

____

____

What 1 or 2 areas of life are you most focused on improving currently? Why and what are you doing to improve them?

Weekly Goals & Habit Tracker

Week Start Date: ____ /____ /________

Goals

- ○ 1. ____
- ○ 2. ____
- ○ 3. ____
- ○ 4. ____

What could get in the way of your goals this week?
Give yourself some words of advice or encouragement.

____

____

Habits	**M**	**T**	**W**	**T**	**F**	**S**	**S**	
____________________	○	○	○	○	○	○	○	___
____________________	○	○	○	○	○	○	○	___
____________________	○	○	○	○	○	○	○	___
____________________	○	○	○	○	○	○	○	___

Grand Total ___

How did the week go? What could you have done better?

____

____

Do you feel the long-term goals you have are ambitious enough? Or maybe too ambitious? How could you improve them?

Weekly Goals & Habit Tracker

Week Start Date: ____ /____ /________

Goals

○ 1. ______________________________

○ 2. ______________________________

○ 3. ______________________________

○ 4. ______________________________

What could get in the way of your goals this week?
Give yourself some words of advice or encouragement.

____

____

Habits	**M**	**T**	**W**	**T**	**F**	**S**	**S**	
________________	○	○	○	○	○	○	○	___
________________	○	○	○	○	○	○	○	___
________________	○	○	○	○	○	○	○	___
________________	○	○	○	○	○	○	○	___

Grand Total ___

How did the week go? What could you have done better?

____

____

Name 1 or 2 traits that you notice in others that you wish you had. Do you plan to work on possibly gaining these traits or just acknowledge that you're different?

____

____

____

____

____

____

____

____

____

____

____

____

____

____

____

____

____

____

____

____

Weekly Goals & Habit Tracker

Week Start Date: ____ /____ /________

Goals

- ○ 1. ______________________________
- ○ 2. ______________________________
- ○ 3. ______________________________
- ○ 4. ______________________________

What could get in the way of your goals this week?
Give yourself some words of advice or encouragement.

____

____

Habits	**M**	**T**	**W**	**T**	**F**	**S**	**S**	
____________	○	○	○	○	○	○	○	___
____________	○	○	○	○	○	○	○	___
____________	○	○	○	○	○	○	○	___
____________	○	○	○	○	○	○	○	___

Grand Total ___

How did the week go? What could you have done better?

____

____

What are 1 or 2 ways you can get out of your comfort zone? This could be something new, scary, fun, or even something nice for someone else.

Weekly Goals & Habit Tracker

Week Start Date: ____/____/________

Goals

- ○ 1. ________________________________
- ○ 2. ________________________________
- ○ 3. ________________________________
- ○ 4. ________________________________

What could get in the way of your goals this week?
Give yourself some words of advice or encouragement.

____

____

Habits	**M**	**T**	**W**	**T**	**F**	**S**	**S**	
________________	○	○	○	○	○	○	○	___
________________	○	○	○	○	○	○	○	___
________________	○	○	○	○	○	○	○	___
________________	○	○	○	○	○	○	○	___

Grand Total ___

How did the week go? What could you have done better?

____

____

Assess your current list of goals. How is your progress? What are some changes you could make to improve that list for next quarter?

Weekly Goals & Habit Tracker

Week Start Date: ____ /____ /________

Goals

○ 1. ____

○ 2. ____

○ 3. ____

○ 4. ____

What could get in the way of your goals this week?
Give yourself some words of advice or encouragement.

____

____

Habits	M	T	W	T	F	S	S	
____________________	○	○	○	○	○	○	○	___
____________________	○	○	○	○	○	○	○	___
____________________	○	○	○	○	○	○	○	___
____________________	○	○	○	○	○	○	○	___

Grand Total ___

How did the week go? What could you have done better?

____

____

If you had to rank the areas of your life (Relationships, Career, Education, Health & Fitness, and Lifestyle) from current highest priority (#1) to lowest priority (#5), how would you rank them?

Weekly Goals & Habit Tracker

Week Start Date: ____ /____ /________

Goals

- ○ 1. ______________________________________
- ○ 2. ______________________________________
- ○ 3. ______________________________________
- ○ 4. ______________________________________

What could get in the way of your goals this week?
Give yourself some words of advice or encouragement.

____

____

Habits	**M**	**T**	**W**	**T**	**F**	**S**	**S**	
____________________	○	○	○	○	○	○	○	___
____________________	○	○	○	○	○	○	○	___
____________________	○	○	○	○	○	○	○	___
____________________	○	○	○	○	○	○	○	___

Grand Total ___

How did the week go? What could you have done better?

____

____

What goal(s) have you been focused on most this quarter? Do you have a plan for your other goals?

Quarter 2

How would you rate your current level of fulfillment in your...

Relationships

Career

Health & Fitness

Education

Lifestyle

What are some ways you could improve the success of your...

Relationships

____

____

____

Career

____

____

____

Health & Fitness

____

____

____

Education

____

____

____

Lifestyle

____

____

____

Write down 20 potential goals:

1. ____

2. ____

3. ____

4. ____

5. ____

6. ____

7. ____

8. ____

9. ____

10. ____

11. ____

12. ____

13. ____

14. ____

15. ____

16. ____

17. ____

18. ____

19. ____

20. ____

And now choose up to 5 to focus on and cross out the rest.

What are your main goals?

Goal #1

____

____

Goal #2

____

____

Goal #3

____

____

Goal #4

____

____

Goal #5

____

____

Weekly Goals & Habit Tracker

Week Start Date: ____ /____ /________

Goals

- O 1. ________________________________
- O 2. ________________________________
- O 3. ________________________________
- O 4. ________________________________

What could get in the way of your goals this week?
Give yourself some words of advice or encouragement.

____

____

Habits	M	T	W	T	F	S	S	
____________	O	O	O	O	O	O	O	___
____________	O	O	O	O	O	O	O	___
____________	O	O	O	O	O	O	O	___
____________	O	O	O	O	O	O	O	___

Grand Total ___

How did the week go? What could you have done better?

____

____

What is 1 mistake you've made in your past? Reflect on what you learned from that.

Weekly Goals & Habit Tracker

Week Start Date: ____ /____ /________

Goals

O 1. ____

O 2. ____

O 3. ____

O 4. ____

What could get in the way of your goals this week?
Give yourself some words of advice or encouragement.

____

____

Habits	M	T	W	T	F	S	S	
____________________	O	O	O	O	O	O	O	___
____________________	O	O	O	O	O	O	O	___
____________________	O	O	O	O	O	O	O	___
____________________	O	O	O	O	O	O	O	___

Grand Total ___

How did the week go? What could you have done better?

____

____

What are a couple things you find yourself complaining about regularly?

*If you find lots of little things bother you more than they should, consider a no-complaint challenge! Aim to go a week or 2 with no complaints. You don't need to count complaints if you make them constructive.

Weekly Goals & Habit Tracker

Week Start Date: ____ /____ /________

Goals

- O 1. ____
- O 2. ____
- O 3. ____
- O 4. ____

What could get in the way of your goals this week?
Give yourself some words of advice or encouragement.

____

____

Habits	M	T	W	T	F	S	S	
____________________	O	O	O	O	O	O	O	___
____________________	O	O	O	O	O	O	O	___
____________________	O	O	O	O	O	O	O	___
____________________	O	O	O	O	O	O	O	___

Grand Total ___

How did the week go? What could you have done better?

____

____

What is one of your greatest fears? What is something you can do to conquer it?

Weekly Goals & Habit Tracker

Week Start Date: ____ /____ /________

Goals

O 1. ____

O 2. ____

O 3. ____

O 4. ____

What could get in the way of your goals this week?
Give yourself some words of advice or encouragement.

____

____

Habits	M	T	W	T	F	S	S	
____________________	O	O	O	O	O	O	O	___
____________________	O	O	O	O	O	O	O	___
____________________	O	O	O	O	O	O	O	___
____________________	O	O	O	O	O	O	O	___

Grand Total ___

How did the week go? What could you have done better?

____

____

What are 1 or 2 traits of 1 or both of your parents that you admire? How about 1 or 2 that you don't? Do you share these traits?

Weekly Goals & Habit Tracker

Week Start Date: ____ /____ /________

Goals

- ○ 1. ____
- ○ 2. ____
- ○ 3. ____
- ○ 4. ____

What could get in the way of your goals this week?
Give yourself some words of advice or encouragement.

____

____

Habits	M	T	W	T	F	S	S	
____________________	○	○	○	○	○	○	○	___
____________________	○	○	○	○	○	○	○	___
____________________	○	○	○	○	○	○	○	___
____________________	○	○	○	○	○	○	○	___

Grand Total ___

How did the week go? What could you have done better?

____

____

What is one vice or bad habit that you have trouble shaking? Be honest with yourself about how detrimental it is.

*If you want to shake a bad habit or vice, try distracting yourself for 5 or 10 minutes with something constructive. You'll likely lose the urge or forget about it completely!

Weekly Goals & Habit Tracker

Week Start Date: ____ /____ /________

Goals

- ○ 1. ______________________________
- ○ 2. ______________________________
- ○ 3. ______________________________
- ○ 4. ______________________________

What could get in the way of your goals this week?
Give yourself some words of advice or encouragement.

____

____

Habits	M	T	W	T	F	S	S	
________________	○	○	○	○	○	○	○	___
________________	○	○	○	○	○	○	○	___
________________	○	○	○	○	○	○	○	___
________________	○	○	○	○	○	○	○	___

Grand Total ___

How did the week go? What could you have done better?

____

____

What are 1 or 2 methods you use to clear your head or to get out of a funk? This could be an activity, music, people, etc.

Weekly Goals & Habit Tracker

Week Start Date: ____ /____ /________

Goals

O 1. ____

O 2. ____

O 3. ____

O 4. ____

What could get in the way of your goals this week?
Give yourself some words of advice or encouragement.

____

____

Habits	M	T	W	T	F	S	S	
____________________	O	O	O	O	O	O	O	___
____________________	O	O	O	O	O	O	O	___
____________________	O	O	O	O	O	O	O	___
____________________	O	O	O	O	O	O	O	___

Grand Total ___

How did the week go? What could you have done better?

____

____

List 2 or 3 major accomplishments you've had in life. How long did it take for you to accomplish those goals and what was the road like to get there? Is there a next step or similar accomplishment you'd like to work toward?

Weekly Goals & Habit Tracker

Week Start Date: ____ /____ /________

Goals

○ 1. ____

○ 2. ____

○ 3. ____

○ 4. ____

What could get in the way of your goals this week?
Give yourself some words of advice or encouragement.

____

____

Habits	M	T	W	T	F	S	S	
____________________	○	○	○	○	○	○	○	___
____________________	○	○	○	○	○	○	○	___
____________________	○	○	○	○	○	○	○	___
____________________	○	○	○	○	○	○	○	___

Grand Total ___

How did the week go? What could you have done better?

____

____

What is one principal that you have related to your relationships?

Weekly Goals & Habit Tracker

Week Start Date: ____ /____ /________

Goals

O 1. ____

O 2. ____

O 3. ____

O 4. ____

What could get in the way of your goals this week?
Give yourself some words of advice or encouragement.

____

____

Habits	**M**	**T**	**W**	**T**	**F**	**S**	**S**	
____________________	O	O	O	O	O	O	O	___
____________________	O	O	O	O	O	O	O	___
____________________	O	O	O	O	O	O	O	___
____________________	O	O	O	O	O	O	O	___

Grand Total ___

How did the week go? What could you have done better?

____

____

Do you feel your life is balanced between working hard and enjoyment? If needed, what can you do to balance that scale?

Weekly Goals & Habit Tracker

Week Start Date: ____ /____ /________

Goals

- ○ 1. ______________________________
- ○ 2. ______________________________
- ○ 3. ______________________________
- ○ 4. ______________________________

What could get in the way of your goals this week?
Give yourself some words of advice or encouragement.

____

____

Habits	M	T	W	T	F	S	S	
____________	○	○	○	○	○	○	○	___
____________	○	○	○	○	○	○	○	___
____________	○	○	○	○	○	○	○	___
____________	○	○	○	○	○	○	○	___

Grand Total ___

How did the week go? What could you have done better?

____

____

Write down at least 10 things in your life you are grateful for.

Weekly Goals & Habit Tracker

Week Start Date: ____ /____ /________

Goals

O 1. ____

O 2. ____

O 3. ____

O 4. ____

What could get in the way of your goals this week?
Give yourself some words of advice or encouragement.

____

____

Habits	**M**	**T**	**W**	**T**	**F**	**S**	**S**	
____________________	O	O	O	O	O	O	O	___
____________________	O	O	O	O	O	O	O	___
____________________	O	O	O	O	O	O	O	___
____________________	O	O	O	O	O	O	O	___

Grand Total ___

How did the week go? What could you have done better?

____

____

Assess your current list of goals. How is your progress? What are some changes you could make to improve that list for next quarter?

____

____

____

____

____

____

____

____

____

____

____

____

____

____

____

____

____

____

____

____

Weekly Goals & Habit Tracker

Week Start Date: ____ /____ /________

Goals

- ○ 1. ____
- ○ 2. ____
- ○ 3. ____
- ○ 4. ____

What could get in the way of your goals this week?
Give yourself some words of advice or encouragement.

____

____

Habits	M	T	W	T	F	S	S	
____________________	○	○	○	○	○	○	○	___
____________________	○	○	○	○	○	○	○	___
____________________	○	○	○	○	○	○	○	___
____________________	○	○	○	○	○	○	○	___

Grand Total ___

How did the week go? What could you have done better?

____

____

If you had to rank the areas of your life (Relationships, Career, Education, Health & Fitness, and Lifestyle) from current highest priority (#1) to lowest priority (#5), how would you rank them?

Weekly Goals & Habit Tracker

Week Start Date: ____ /____ /________

Goals

○ 1. ____

○ 2. ____

○ 3. ____

○ 4. ____

What could get in the way of your goals this week?
Give yourself some words of advice or encouragement.

____

____

Habits	**M**	**T**	**W**	**T**	**F**	**S**	**S**	
____________________	○	○	○	○	○	○	○	___
____________________	○	○	○	○	○	○	○	___
____________________	○	○	○	○	○	○	○	___
____________________	○	○	○	○	○	○	○	___

Grand Total ___

How did the week go? What could you have done better?

____

____

What goal(s) have you been focused on most this quarter? Do you have a plan for your other goals?

Share Your Thoughts!

I just want to take a quick break to ask you to share your thoughts! You can do that in 1 of 3 ways:

1. If you've found this journal valuable, you can share this journal with someone who may also get value from it. Send them the Amazon link or surprise them with the journal as a gift!
2. This journal is only sold on Amazon.com. That being said, reviews are extremely helpful so that others can find it. All I ask is that you give an honest review.
3. Email me directly at twelvepathsnews@gmail.com. Let me know what you like and what improvements can be made. I'm also interested to hear what types of goals and habits have helped you the most!

Thank you ahead of time – I look forward to hearing from you!

Quarter 3

How would you rate your current level of fulfillment in your...

Relationships

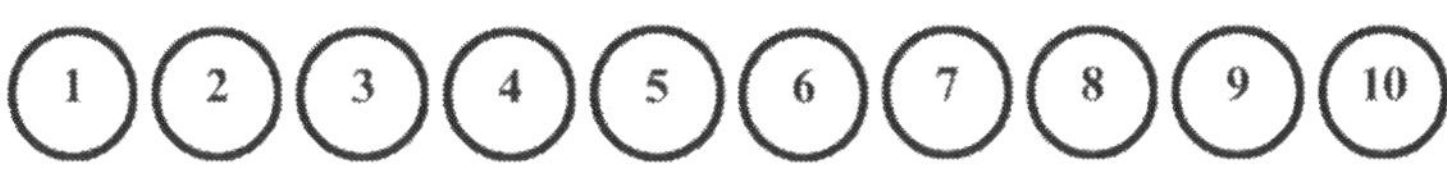

Career

Health & Fitness

Education

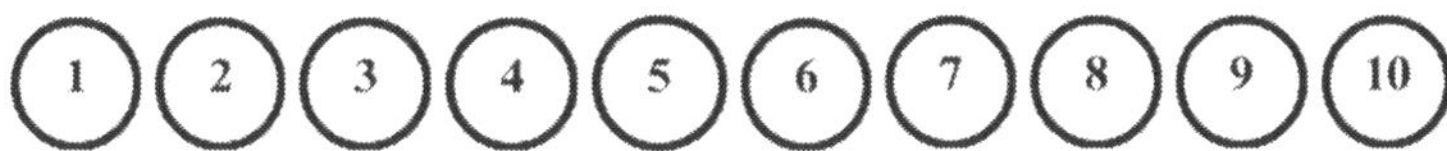

Lifestyle

What are some ways you could improve the success of your…

Relationships

____

____

____

Career

____

____

____

Health & Fitness

____

____

____

Education

____

____

____

Lifestyle

____

____

____

Write down 20 potential goals:

1. ______________________________

2. ______________________________

3. ______________________________

4. ______________________________

5. ______________________________

6. ______________________________

7. ______________________________

8. ______________________________

9. ______________________________

10. ______________________________

11. ______________________________

12. ______________________________

13. ______________________________

14. ______________________________

15. ______________________________

16. ______________________________

17. ______________________________

18. ______________________________

19. ______________________________

20. ______________________________

And now choose up to 5 to focus on and cross out the rest.

What are your main goals?

Goal #1

____

____

Goal #2

____

____

Goal #3

____

____

Goal #4

____

____

Goal #5

____

____

Weekly Goals & Habit Tracker

Week Start Date: ____ /____ /________

Goals

- ○ 1. ________________________________
- ○ 2. ________________________________
- ○ 3. ________________________________
- ○ 4. ________________________________

What could get in the way of your goals this week?
Give yourself some words of advice or encouragement.

____

____

Habits	**M**	**T**	**W**	**T**	**F**	**S**	**S**	
____________	○	○	○	○	○	○	○	___
____________	○	○	○	○	○	○	○	___
____________	○	○	○	○	○	○	○	___
____________	○	○	○	○	○	○	○	___

Grand Total ___

How did the week go? What could you have done better?

____

____

Who are 1 or 2 of the most positive people in your life to be around? What about them makes them so positive?

Weekly Goals & Habit Tracker

Week Start Date: ____ /____ /________

Goals

○ 1. ________________________________

○ 2. ________________________________

○ 3. ________________________________

○ 4. ________________________________

What could get in the way of your goals this week?
Give yourself some words of advice or encouragement.

____

____

Habits	M	T	W	T	F	S	S	
________________	○	○	○	○	○	○	○	___
________________	○	○	○	○	○	○	○	___
________________	○	○	○	○	○	○	○	___
________________	○	○	○	○	○	○	○	___

Grand Total ___

How did the week go? What could you have done better?

____

____

Reflect about a time where you had a near death experience or someone close to you died or had a near miss.

Weekly Goals & Habit Tracker

Week Start Date: ____ /____ /________

Goals

- O 1. ____
- O 2. ____
- O 3. ____
- O 4. ____

What could get in the way of your goals this week?
Give yourself some words of advice or encouragement.

____

____

Habits	M	T	W	T	F	S	S	
____________________	O	O	O	O	O	O	O	___
____________________	O	O	O	O	O	O	O	___
____________________	O	O	O	O	O	O	O	___
____________________	O	O	O	O	O	O	O	___

Grand Total ___

How did the week go? What could you have done better?

____

____

What's the last nice, noteworthy thing you've done for someone else?

Weekly Goals & Habit Tracker

Week Start Date: ____ /____ /________

Goals

O 1. ____

O 2. ____

O 3. ____

O 4. ____

What could get in the way of your goals this week?
Give yourself some words of advice or encouragement.

____

____

Habits	M	T	W	T	F	S	S	
____________________	O	O	O	O	O	O	O	___
____________________	O	O	O	O	O	O	O	___
____________________	O	O	O	O	O	O	O	___
____________________	O	O	O	O	O	O	O	___

Grand Total ___

How did the week go? What could you have done better?

____

____

What is are some activities you'd like to at least give a try? What has been in the way of trying these things?

____

____

____

____

____

____

____

____

____

____

____

____

____

____

____

____

____

____

____

____

____

Weekly Goals & Habit Tracker

Week Start Date: ____ /____ /________

Goals

- ○ 1. ______________________________
- ○ 2. ______________________________
- ○ 3. ______________________________
- ○ 4. ______________________________

What could get in the way of your goals this week?
Give yourself some words of advice or encouragement.

____

____

Habits	M	T	W	T	F	S	S	
____________________	○	○	○	○	○	○	○	___
____________________	○	○	○	○	○	○	○	___
____________________	○	○	○	○	○	○	○	___
____________________	○	○	○	○	○	○	○	___

Grand Total ___

How did the week go? What could you have done better?

____

____

What is 1 excuse that you tell yourself often? What would happen if you quit telling yourself that excuse?

Weekly Goals & Habit Tracker

Week Start Date: ____ /____ /________

Goals

O 1. ____

O 2. ____

O 3. ____

O 4. ____

What could get in the way of your goals this week?
Give yourself some words of advice or encouragement.

____

____

Habits	**M**	**T**	**W**	**T**	**F**	**S**	**S**	
____________________	O	O	O	O	O	O	O	___
____________________	O	O	O	O	O	O	O	___
____________________	O	O	O	O	O	O	O	___
____________________	O	O	O	O	O	O	O	___

Grand Total ___

How did the week go? What could you have done better?

____

____

Do you enjoy your current job and are you excited for where your career path is taking you? If yes, why? And if no, why haven't you found a new opportunity?

Weekly Goals & Habit Tracker

Week Start Date: ____ /____ /________

Goals

O 1. ______________________________

O 2. ______________________________

O 3. ______________________________

O 4. ______________________________

What could get in the way of your goals this week?
Give yourself some words of advice or encouragement.

____

____

Habits	M	T	W	T	F	S	S	
____________	O	O	O	O	O	O	O	___
____________	O	O	O	O	O	O	O	___
____________	O	O	O	O	O	O	O	___
____________	O	O	O	O	O	O	O	___

Grand Total ___

How did the week go? What could you have done better?

____

____

Who are 3 people that you look up to? Why?

Weekly Goals & Habit Tracker

Week Start Date: ____ /____ /________

Goals

O 1. ____

O 2. ____

O 3. ____

O 4. ____

What could get in the way of your goals this week?
Give yourself some words of advice or encouragement.

____

____

Habits	M	T	W	T	F	S	S	
________________________	O	O	O	O	O	O	O	___
________________________	O	O	O	O	O	O	O	___
________________________	O	O	O	O	O	O	O	___
________________________	O	O	O	O	O	O	O	___

Grand Total ____

How did the week go? What could you have done better?

____

____

What goal(s) or idea(s) do you have in mind that makes you feel ambitious?

Weekly Goals & Habit Tracker

Week Start Date: ____ /____ /________

Goals

O 1. ____

O 2. ____

O 3. ____

O 4. ____

What could get in the way of your goals this week?
Give yourself some words of advice or encouragement.

____

____

Habits	M	T	W	T	F	S	S	
____________________	O	O	O	O	O	O	O	___
____________________	O	O	O	O	O	O	O	___
____________________	O	O	O	O	O	O	O	___
____________________	O	O	O	O	O	O	O	___

Grand Total ___

How did the week go? What could you have done better?

____

____

What does your current exercise routine look like? Could it use improvement and if so, how?

Weekly Goals & Habit Tracker

Week Start Date: ____ /____ /________

Goals

- ○ 1. ____
- ○ 2. ____
- ○ 3. ____
- ○ 4. ____

What could get in the way of your goals this week?
Give yourself some words of advice or encouragement.

____

____

Habits	M	T	W	T	F	S	S	
____________________	○	○	○	○	○	○	○	___
____________________	○	○	○	○	○	○	○	___
____________________	○	○	○	○	○	○	○	___
____________________	○	○	○	○	○	○	○	___

Grand Total ___

How did the week go? What could you have done better?

____

____

What are 1 or 2 accomplishments from the past 5 years that you are proud of?

Weekly Goals & Habit Tracker

Week Start Date: ____/____/________

Goals

- ○ 1. ______________________________
- ○ 2. ______________________________
- ○ 3. ______________________________
- ○ 4. ______________________________

What could get in the way of your goals this week?
Give yourself some words of advice or encouragement.

____

____

Habits	M	T	W	T	F	S	S	
______________	○	○	○	○	○	○	○	___
______________	○	○	○	○	○	○	○	___
______________	○	○	○	○	○	○	○	___
______________	○	○	○	○	○	○	○	___

Grand Total ___

How did the week go? What could you have done better?

____

____

Assess your current list of goals. How is your progress? What are some changes you could make to improve that list for next quarter?

Weekly Goals & Habit Tracker

Week Start Date: ____ /____ /________

Goals

- ○ 1. ______________________________
- ○ 2. ______________________________
- ○ 3. ______________________________
- ○ 4. ______________________________

What could get in the way of your goals this week?
Give yourself some words of advice or encouragement.

____

____

Habits	M	T	W	T	F	S	S	
____________	○	○	○	○	○	○	○	___
____________	○	○	○	○	○	○	○	___
____________	○	○	○	○	○	○	○	___
____________	○	○	○	○	○	○	○	___

Grand Total ___

How did the week go? What could you have done better?

____

____

If you had to rank the areas of your life (Relationships, Career, Education, Health & Fitness, and Lifestyle) from current highest priority (#1) to lowest priority (#5), how would you rank them?

Weekly Goals & Habit Tracker

Week Start Date: ____ /____ /________

Goals

○ 1. ____

○ 2. ____

○ 3. ____

○ 4. ____

What could get in the way of your goals this week?
Give yourself some words of advice or encouragement.

____

____

Habits	M	T	W	T	F	S	S	
____________________	○	○	○	○	○	○	○	___
____________________	○	○	○	○	○	○	○	___
____________________	○	○	○	○	○	○	○	___
____________________	○	○	○	○	○	○	○	___

Grand Total ___

How did the week go? What could you have done better?

____

____

What goal(s) have you been focused on most this quarter? Do you have a plan for your other goals?

Quarter 4

How would you rate your current level of fulfillment in your…

Relationships

Career

Health & Fitness

Education

Lifestyle

What are some ways you could improve the success of your…

Relationships

____

____

____

Career

____

____

____

Health & Fitness

____

____

____

Education

____

____

____

Lifestyle

____

____

____

Write down 20 potential goals:

1. ____

2. ____

3. ____

4. ____

5. ____

6. ____

7. ____

8. ____

9. ____

10. ____

11. ____

12. ____

13. ____

14. ____

15. ____

16. ____

17. ____

18. ____

19. ____

20. ____

And now choose up to 5 to focus on and cross out the rest.

What are your main goals?

Goal #1

____

____

Goal #2

____

____

Goal #3

____

____

Goal #4

____

____

Goal #5

____

____

Weekly Goals & Habit Tracker

Week Start Date: ____ /____ /________

Goals

- O 1. ______________________________
- O 2. ______________________________
- O 3. ______________________________
- O 4. ______________________________

What could get in the way of your goals this week?
Give yourself some words of advice or encouragement.

____

____

Habits	M	T	W	T	F	S	S	
______________	O	O	O	O	O	O	O	___
______________	O	O	O	O	O	O	O	___
______________	O	O	O	O	O	O	O	___
______________	O	O	O	O	O	O	O	___

Grand Total ___

How did the week go? What could you have done better?

____

____

Do you currently focus more on working hard or on enjoying life? Do you feel you need to adjust focus?

Weekly Goals & Habit Tracker

Week Start Date: ____/____/________

Goals

- ○ 1. ____
- ○ 2. ____
- ○ 3. ____
- ○ 4. ____

What could get in the way of your goals this week?
Give yourself some words of advice or encouragement.

____

____

Habits	**M**	**T**	**W**	**T**	**F**	**S**	**S**	
____________________	○	○	○	○	○	○	○	___
____________________	○	○	○	○	○	○	○	___
____________________	○	○	○	○	○	○	○	___
____________________	○	○	○	○	○	○	○	___

Grand Total ___

How did the week go? What could you have done better?

____

____

What's a principal that you live by that's related to your lifestyle?

Weekly Goals & Habit Tracker

Week Start Date: ____ /____ /________

Goals

O 1. ______________________________

O 2. ______________________________

O 3. ______________________________

O 4. ______________________________

What could get in the way of your goals this week?
Give yourself some words of advice or encouragement.

____

____

Habits	M	T	W	T	F	S	S	
____________	O	O	O	O	O	O	O	___
____________	O	O	O	O	O	O	O	___
____________	O	O	O	O	O	O	O	___
____________	O	O	O	O	O	O	O	___

Grand Total ___

How did the week go? What could you have done better?

____

____

If you could have dinner or a conversation with 1 person (alive or dead), who would it be and why?

Weekly Goals & Habit Tracker

Week Start Date: ____ /____ /________

Goals

○ 1. ____

○ 2. ____

○ 3. ____

○ 4. ____

What could get in the way of your goals this week?
Give yourself some words of advice or encouragement.

____

____

Habits	M	T	W	T	F	S	S	
____________________	○	○	○	○	○	○	○	___
____________________	○	○	○	○	○	○	○	___
____________________	○	○	○	○	○	○	○	___
____________________	○	○	○	○	○	○	○	___

Grand Total ___

How did the week go? What could you have done better?

____

____

Recall a memory that has had a lasting impact on who you are.

Weekly Goals & Habit Tracker

Week Start Date: ____ /____ /________

Goals

- ○ 1. ______________________________
- ○ 2. ______________________________
- ○ 3. ______________________________
- ○ 4. ______________________________

What could get in the way of your goals this week?
Give yourself some words of advice or encouragement.

____

____

Habits	M	T	W	T	F	S	S	
______________	○	○	○	○	○	○	○	___
______________	○	○	○	○	○	○	○	___
______________	○	○	○	○	○	○	○	___
______________	○	○	○	○	○	○	○	___

Grand Total ___

How did the week go? What could you have done better?

____

____

If you won 10 million dollars, what would you plan to do with it? Would your overall lifestyle change?

Weekly Goals & Habit Tracker

Week Start Date: ____ /____ /________

Goals

- O 1. ____
- O 2. ____
- O 3. ____
- O 4. ____

What could get in the way of your goals this week?
Give yourself some words of advice or encouragement.

____

____

Habits	M	T	W	T	F	S	S	
____________________	O	O	O	O	O	O	O	___
____________________	O	O	O	O	O	O	O	___
____________________	O	O	O	O	O	O	O	___
____________________	O	O	O	O	O	O	O	___

Grand Total ___

How did the week go? What could you have done better?

____

____

If you had to sum up your overall philosophy of life in one phrase, what would it be?

Weekly Goals & Habit Tracker

Week Start Date: ____ /____ /________

Goals

O 1. ____

O 2. ____

O 3. ____

O 4. ____

What could get in the way of your goals this week?
Give yourself some words of advice or encouragement.

____

____

Habits	M	T	W	T	F	S	S	
____________________	O	O	O	O	O	O	O	___
____________________	O	O	O	O	O	O	O	___
____________________	O	O	O	O	O	O	O	___
____________________	O	O	O	O	O	O	O	___

Grand Total ___

How did the week go? What could you have done better?

____

____

What is something coming up in the next year that you're looking forward to? What about it excites you?

Weekly Goals & Habit Tracker

Week Start Date: ____ /____ /________

Goals

- ○ 1. ________________________________
- ○ 2. ________________________________
- ○ 3. ________________________________
- ○ 4. ________________________________

What could get in the way of your goals this week?
Give yourself some words of advice or encouragement.

____

____

Habits	**M**	**T**	**W**	**T**	**F**	**S**	**S**	
____________	○	○	○	○	○	○	○	___
____________	○	○	○	○	○	○	○	___
____________	○	○	○	○	○	○	○	___
____________	○	○	○	○	○	○	○	___

Grand Total ___

How did the week go? What could you have done better?

____

____

What are a couple words that friends or family have used to describe you? Do you enjoy having these traits?

Weekly Goals & Habit Tracker

Week Start Date: ____/____/________

Goals

O 1. ____

O 2. ____

O 3. ____

O 4. ____

What could get in the way of your goals this week?
Give yourself some words of advice or encouragement.

____

____

Habits	M	T	W	T	F	S	S	
____________________	O	O	O	O	O	O	O	___
____________________	O	O	O	O	O	O	O	___
____________________	O	O	O	O	O	O	O	___
____________________	O	O	O	O	O	O	O	___

Grand Total ___

How did the week go? What could you have done better?

____

____

Name 2 mentors you've had in your life and reflect on what you've learned from them.

Weekly Goals & Habit Tracker

Week Start Date: ____ /____ /________

Goals

- O 1. ______________________________
- O 2. ______________________________
- O 3. ______________________________
- O 4. ______________________________

What could get in the way of your goals this week?
Give yourself some words of advice or encouragement.

____

____

Habits	M	T	W	T	F	S	S	
____________	O	O	O	O	O	O	O	___
____________	O	O	O	O	O	O	O	___
____________	O	O	O	O	O	O	O	___
____________	O	O	O	O	O	O	O	___

Grand Total ___

How did the week go? What could you have done better?

____

____

How do you feel about what you were able to accomplish over this past year?

Weekly Goals & Habit Tracker

Week Start Date: ____ /____ /________

Goals

○ 1. ____

○ 2. ____

○ 3. ____

○ 4. ____

What could get in the way of your goals this week?
Give yourself some words of advice or encouragement.

____

____

Habits	M	T	W	T	F	S	S	
____________________	○	○	○	○	○	○	○	___
____________________	○	○	○	○	○	○	○	___
____________________	○	○	○	○	○	○	○	___
____________________	○	○	○	○	○	○	○	___

Grand Total ___

How did the week go? What could you have done better?

____

____

Assess your current list of goals. How is your progress? What are some changes you could make to improve that list for next quarter?

Weekly Goals & Habit Tracker

Week Start Date: ____ /____ /________

Goals

- O 1. ________________________________
- O 2. ________________________________
- O 3. ________________________________
- O 4. ________________________________

What could get in the way of your goals this week?
Give yourself some words of advice or encouragement.

____

____

Habits	M	T	W	T	F	S	S	
____________	O	O	O	O	O	O	O	___
____________	O	O	O	O	O	O	O	___
____________	O	O	O	O	O	O	O	___
____________	O	O	O	O	O	O	O	___

Grand Total ___

How did the week go? What could you have done better?

____

____

What goal(s) have you been focused on most this quarter? Do you have a plan for your other goals?

Weekly Goals & Habit Tracker

Week Start Date: ____ /____ /________

Goals

O 1. ____

O 2. ____

O 3. ____

O 4. ____

What could get in the way of your goals this week?
Give yourself some words of advice or encouragement.

____

____

Habits	M	T	W	T	F	S	S	
____________________	O	O	O	O	O	O	O	___
____________________	O	O	O	O	O	O	O	___
____________________	O	O	O	O	O	O	O	___
____________________	O	O	O	O	O	O	O	___

Grand Total ___

How did the week go? What could you have done better?

____

____

If you had to rank the areas of your life (Relationships, Career, Education, Health & Fitness, and Lifestyle) from current highest priority (#1) to lowest priority (#5), how would you rank them?

Thank You & Congrats!

Congratulations for getting through a full year of this journal! I hope you've found it helpful to track your habits and goals and that it has allowed you to accomplish things you may not have without it. All the credit for those accomplishments goes to you.

It's my pleasure to have been able to assist you. Thank you for using this journal. If you have any feedback, positive or constructive, I'd love to hear it. You can email me directly at twelvepathsnews@gmail.com.

If you'd like to be in-the-know about updates to this journal or other projects of mine, head to www.twelvepaths.com. There you can subscribe to my email list.

Lastly, if you make your way to Amazon for your next copy, please leave a review while you are there. It helps this journal reach more people and it means the world to me.

Thank you! ☺

Open Journal

Made in the USA
Columbia, SC
14 April 2024

6fd3af7f-f57e-4c5b-9627-8c0c44439b25R01